A Little Bit

of

Common Sense

Addressed to the Inhabitants of America

2017 Pamphlet

written by John Masella

Masella, John
A Little Bit of Common Sense

*Cover design by
Adelia Masella, 4 Corners Design*

ISBN: 978-1724928603

CONTENTS

A Little Bit of Common Sense
Addressed to the Inhabitants of America

SEAL OF THE UNITED STATES OF AMERICA
NH
G
SC
RI
NC
C
V
NY
M
NJ
DC
P
E PLURIBUS UNUM
MDOCLXXVI.

A Little Bit of Common Sense

Addressed to the Inhabitants of America

Despair, despair ~ politically the country is being run by a gang of incompetent, irresponsible, morons.
Our government isn't working.

Last year my Dream was a new constitutional convention ~ a multi-party parliamentary government like the rest of the civilized world. I was so much younger then, I'm older than that now.

I've designed a new constitution ~ more conservative, in some ways, but more responsible. And no, it can't/won't happen, but heck it's my dream ~ if you don't like it make your own dream ~ or enjoy/despair with the status quo!

2017

Written by John Masella

Taking a cue from James Madison's original
Virginia Plan [1787] and repealing
the 17th Amendment ~ guidelines for the ~

New Constitution

- gerrymandering all districts abolished

- all elective offices limited to one four~year term
  [ever]

- all political primaries abolished

- all elections publicly financed ~ six~week
  campaign

- Federal system revamped ~ Electoral College
  eliminated

THE SEAL OF
CONTRA COSTA COUNTY CALIFORNIA

New Constitution
State Assembly

State Counties ~ basic political unit

- each county has a minimum of one assemblyman

State Assembly consists of 400 members divided proportionally by population to the counties

The Assembly is elected as a Body to serve
One term of Four years

- any county citizen resident with 400 signatures can run for assemblyman in a six~week publicly financed election

- at the end of the Assembly's Term it elects 100 State Senators from its Body for the new senate

- before it adjoins, the Assembly conducts an orientation for the New Assembly members

New Constitution State Senate

The State Senate is elected by the State Assembly
as a Body

- the 100 members serve One term of Four years

- the State Senate elects Congressional
  Representatives

- from its membership, it nominates
  Two candidates for Governor

- at the end of its term; six-week campaign;
  publicly financed

- the elected Governor [one four-year term]
  chooses the Lt. Governor and all political
  appointments from the lame duck Senate

- at the end of its term, the Senate conducts an
  orientation for the new State Senate

New Constitution
House of
Representatives

The State Senates elect the 400 members of the House as a single Body at the same time

- the House is proportionally based on population

- each state has at least one representative

- the House as a Body serves One four-year term [Congressmen are limited to one term]

- at the end of the term the House elects 100 Senators [not by states] from the membership

- the House conducts an orientation for the new Congressmen at the end of the Term

New Constitution
The Senate

The House of Representatives elects the Senate from the members of the Body at the same time

- the 100 Senators serve One term of Four years as a Body [not by states]
- at the end of the Term the Senate nominates Two candidates for President from the membership Body
- the Senate conducts an orientation for the new Senate at the end of the Term

SEAL OF THE PRESIDENT OF THE UNITED STATES
E PLURIBUS UNUM

New Constitution
The President

Two Senators are nominated and elected by the Senate to campaign for President

- six-week campaign publicly financed

- the President is elected by National popular vote

- the elected President selects the Vice President; Cabinet; appointees; from the lame duck Senate

- the President is limited to One four-year Term

- the President conducts an orientation for the new President elect

- at the End of the Term of office the President becomes a Supreme Court Justice for life

- the Justice serving the longest time on the bench is Chief Justice

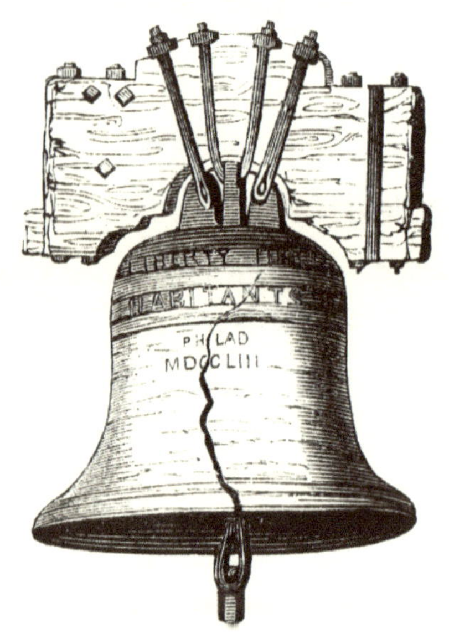

INHABITANTS
PHILAD
MDCCLIII

New Constitution Summation

This design of a new constitution is a political process. The new government will use all the: rules/regulations.; protocols; mechanics; of the old government until they can be: eliminated; repealed; modified.

Every Four years the citizens of the Nation
will vote for:

Assemblyman ~ Governor ~ President

HONORIUM LADDER

- Citizens elect: Assemblymen
- Assemblymen elect: State Senators
- State Senators elect: Governor candidates
- State Senators elect: Congressmen
- Congressmen elect: Senators
- Senators elect: Presidential candidates
- Presidents become: Supreme Court Justices

ANNUIT CŒPTIS
MDCCLXXVI.
NOVUS ORDO SECLORUM

New Constitution
Conclusion

Power of political Parties ~ diminished

- lobbying and big money influencing the political process ~ illegal
- removal of entrenched political power
- a fluid political process whereby every four years new, fresh faces in government
- a winnowing/funneling design for civic/virtuous citizens to become leaders

Afterward

The author, my brother, being two years older, taught me everything as a kid. When I was 6 years old, he taught me to memorize the order and names of all the planets in our solar system and taught me what that meant as well. We would spend hours drawing rocket ships, I always copied his, so sleek and fast looking. They looked like what my Prius Prime looks like today. Space X rockets pale in comparison. The rockets of today have nothing on my brother's drawings at 8 years old. He continues to teach me till this very day.

His mind visualizes other worlds, different possibilities, other ways of looking at things that no one else seems to see. A student, and master, of history, his sense of the lives of nations is deep and wide. What we see today, is not what tomorrow will bring, even with the repetition of the mistakes of history.

What if we reconceptualize democracy? The form of our government today was an experiment. And it held reasonably well until just recently. It is telling that all the broken countries that we tried to fix after all the wars we've waged turned to Parliamentary governments, not representative ones like our own. We could have written their new constitutions identically to ours, yet we chose not to. What does this tell us about our own government that wrote the rules for other countries?

Our form of government is fraught with problems today. A president elected by electors (a species of being rarely seen in public) over the objections of the majority of the populace. A bicameral Congress where a state of 600 thousand plus population has two senators as does the largest state with nearly 40 million. Odd, isn't it? No matter, because the Congress has crawled to an impassable standstill anyway, the political divide too difficult to cross. The third governing body meant to check the excesses of politics, the supreme court, packed with political appointees, decrees by political platform rather than judicial review.

The time has come to rethink our form of democracy. How can we make citizen elections work along with maintaining specialized governmental knowledge and understanding of how to get things done and simply run well?

That time and that concept is drawn up in this pamphlet.

With a tip of the hat to Thomas Paine for getting things started, John Masella, my brother, takes it one step forward.

Dennis Masella

Notes